THIS BOOK BELONGS TO:

_____

TODAY'S DATE:

_____

101 *Great* THINGS GOD SAYS ABOUT YOU

101 Great Things God Says About You: Faith Reminders When You Need Them Most

Copyright © 2025 Joel Osteen

All rights reserved. No part of this book may be reproduced or transmitted in any form or by any means, electronic or mechanical, including photocopying, recording, or by any information storage and retrieval system, without permission in writing from the publisher.

Unless otherwise noted, scripture quotations are taken from the *Holy Bible*, New Living Translation, copyright © 1996, 2004, 2015 by Tyndale House Foundation. Used by permission of Tyndale House Publishers, Carol Stream, Illinois 60188. All rights reserved.

Scripture quotations marked ESV are taken from The ESV® Bible (The Holy Bible, English Standard Version®), © 2001 by Crossway, a publishing ministry of Good News Publishers. All rights reserved.

Scripture quotations marked NIV are taken from the Holy Bible, New International Version®, NIV®. Copyright © 1973, 1978, 1984, 2011 by Biblica, Inc.™ Used by permission of Zondervan. All rights reserved worldwide. www.zondervan.com The "NIV" and "New International Version" are trademarks registered in the United States Patent and Trademark Office by Biblica, Inc.™

Scripture quotations marked NKJV are taken from the New King James Version®. Copyright © 1982 by Thomas Nelson. Used by permission. All rights reserved.

Scripture quotations marked TLB are taken from *The Living Bible*, copyright © 1971 by Tyndale House Foundation. Used by permission of Tyndale House Publishers, Carol Stream, Illinois 60188.
All rights reserved.

Scripture quotations marked TPT are taken from The Passion Translation®. Copyright © 2017, 2018, 2020 by Passion & Fire Ministries, Inc. Used by permission. All rights reserved. ThePassionTranslation.com.

ISBN: 978-1-963492-26-2

Created and assembled for Joel Osteen Ministries by
Breakfast for Seven
breakfastforseven.com

Printed in China.

For additional resources by Joel Osteen, visit JoelOsteen.com

101 *Great* THINGS GOD SAYS ABOUT YOU

JOEL OSTEEN

Faith reminders when you need them most

How to Use This Book:

It's Time to Believe Every Word *He Says About You.*

All of us are confronted with lies we have to choose whether to believe or not, and sometimes you just need a reminder of the great things God says about you. Use this book as a resource to encourage your heart and remind you of who you are in Him.

01 Find it.
Search by the topic that is on your heart.

02 Believe it.
Read the corresponding scripture and believe in your heart that what God says about you is true.

03 Speak it.
Now that you believe the truth, speak it out! Say it loud and confident over yourself.

Plus... detach the poster at the back of this book to declare these reminders every day.

Table of Contents

God Says You Are:

01	**You are known**	15
02	**You are forgiven**	17
03	**You are extraordinary**	19
04	**You are a new creation**	21
05	**You are never alone**	23
06	**You are free**	25
07	**You are loved**	27
08	**You are secure in God's love**	29
09	**You are strong**	31
10	**You are a temple of the Holy Spirit**	33
11	**You are chosen**	35
12	**You are both valuable and worthy**	37
13	**You are God's masterpiece**	39
14	**You are precious**	41
15	**You are empowered**	43
16	**You are a friend of God**	45

17	You are an heir with Christ	47
18	You are a child of God and have been adopted into God's family	49
19	You are God's favorite	51
20	You are redeemed	53
21	You are more than a conqueror	55
22	You are kept safe	57
23	You are blessed with every spiritual blessing	59
24	You are the head — not the tail	61
25	You are a significant part of the body of Christ	63
26	You are a royal priesthood	65
27	You are healed	67
28	You are a citizen of Heaven	69
29	You are provided for	71
30	You are a servant	73
31	You are a partaker of the divine nature	75
32	You are a witness	77

There is so much more . . .

Keep going . . .

33	**You are justified**	79
34	**You are making a difference**	81
35	**You are being sanctified**	83
36	**You are an ambassador for Christ**	85
37	**You are cared for**	87
38	**You are blessed to be a blessing**	89
39	**You are a branch of the vine**	91
40	**You are covered by God's grace**	93
41	**You are made in the image of God**	95
42	**You are able to hear God's voice**	97
43	**You are an overcomer of fear**	99
44	**You are victorious**	101
45	**You are anointed**	103
46	**You are here for such a time as this**	105
47	**You are a recipient of God's compassion**	107
48	**You are given a future filled with hope**	109
49	**You are pure**	111
50	**You are equipped for every good work**	113

51	You are covered by God's wings and are shielded from the enemy	117
52	You are a part of the new covenant	119
53	You are a recipient of eternal life	121
54	You are given a spirit of power, love, and self-discipline	123
55	You are not late	125
56	You are promised peace of mind	127
57	You are complete in Christ	129
58	You are heard	131
59	You are highly favored	133
60	You are surrounded by God's goodness	135
61	You are a mighty hero	137
62	You are a light of the world	139
63	You are sustained by God	141
64	You are promised rest	143
65	You are free from condemnation	145
66	You are God's treasured possession	147

His love goes on and on . . .

Almost there! . . .

67	**You are not alone in your struggles**	149
68	**You are being transformed**	151
69	**You are blessed when you persevere**	153
70	**You are welcomed into His presence**	155
71	**You are a co-worker with God**	157
72	**You are held in God's hands**	159
73	**You are a beacon of hope to others**	161
74	**You are a valuable part of your community**	163
75	**You are part of God's divine plan**	165
76	**You are creative**	167
77	**You are a warrior**	169
78	**You are chosen to bear fruit and be fruitful**	171
79	**You are a joy to God**	173
80	**You are guided by the Lord**	175
81	**You are meant to thrive and not just survive**	177
82	**You are destined for greatness**	179
83	**You are strengthened in weakness**	181
84	**You are given wisdom**	183

85	You are not defined by your past	185
86	You are righteous	187
87	You are given the mind of Christ	189
88	You are surrounded by God's presence	191
89	You are storing up treasures in Heaven	193
90	You are a source of encouragement to others	195
91	You are given new mercies every day	197
92	You are being renewed day by day	199
93	You are both courageous and brave	201
94	You are a recipient of God's promises	203
95	You are beautiful	205
96	You are uniquely talented, gifted, and skilled	207
97	You are lacking nothing	209
98	You are a work in progress	211
99	You are enough	213
100	You are accepted	215
101	You are growing every day	217

Believe it. Speak It!

Introduction

All of us have tough days. We encounter circumstances that wear us down or damage our self-esteem. We have thoughts that contradict who God says we are. Too often we let our trauma or environment dictate our identity. And it's certainly tempting to let the worldly voices win, but God did not create you to live insecure, unsure, fearful, lacking, or defeated. He created you in His image and with intentional purpose, and He is the only One who can determine your identity. In His Word, God shares all you need to know about who He says you are. No one can refute it or change it. The Most High God, your Creator, has the final word. And He says you are . . .

Known. Loved. Victorious. A new creation. A child of God. Chosen. Forgiven. Meant to thrive. Destined for greatness. Blessed. Pure. Given the mind of Christ. Free. Empowered. Provided for. Precious.

The list goes on, and every bit of it is true about you.

It's possible to go through your entire life and not really know who you are. Don't let that be your story. Don't let the enemy label you or distort how you see yourself. The wrong identity will hinder you from becoming who you were created to be. It's time to live in alignment with what Almighty God says about you. With these reminders, I believe and declare that you will step into a new awareness of who you are in Christ. Chains will break, doors will open, and you will walk with confidence in the fullness of your destiny.

Joel Osteen

01 You are *known.*

Look to His Word:

"I knew you before I formed you in your mother's womb. Before you were born I set you apart and appointed you as my prophet to the nations."

JEREMIAH 1:5

See it for yourself:

Before the foundation of the earth, you were on God's mind. He was there when you were formed in your mother's womb. He knows every hair on your head and every word you've ever said. He knows the details of your victories and your mistakes. He knows your deepest fears and regrets — the ones you won't speak to anyone. He knows what makes you smile and gives you joy. He knows your ups and your downs. He sees your potential, and He's equipped you to do great things. You don't have to worry about being misunderstood with Him because He sees your heart and your intentions. He knows who you are at your very core, and He loves you. You are no stranger to Him — you have been brought into His family, and you are known inside and out.

02 You are *forgiven.*

Look to His Word:

But if we confess our sins to him, he is faithful and just to forgive us our sins and to cleanse us from all wickedness.

1 JOHN 1:9

See it for yourself:

We all do things we know we shouldn't, but God's grace is bigger than any mistake or failure. It doesn't matter what you've done or how far you've strayed; if you confess to Him, He is faithful and just to forgive you. Don't let the enemy accuse you or tell you you're unworthy. Refuse to believe the enemy's lies right now. You are not perfect, but you are forgiven. Your sins have been washed away, and you have been made holy through Christ's sacrifice (Hebrews 10:10). You don't have to drag yesterday's mistakes into today or carry the weight of guilt and shame. You don't have to carry around baggage filled with regret. Unload it all to God. His mercies are fresh every morning, and your sins are forgotten, removed as far as the east is from the west (Psalm 103:12). In Christ you are forgiven.

03

You are
extraordinary.

Look to His Word:

I will praise You, for I am fearfully
and wonderfully made; marvelous are
Your works, and that my soul knows very well.

PSALM 139:14 (NKJV)

See it for yourself:

There is no one like you in the whole world! No one else has your fingerprints. No one else has your mind or personality or destiny. No one else can do what you can do. You're not common. You didn't come off an assembly line. You weren't mass-produced. You're not ordinary — you are extraordinary. God created you with purpose and intentionality to be special and unique. He doesn't want you to try to be like someone else — He wants you to be who He created you to be. He loves every little thing about you. You are fearfully and wonderfully made, just as you are. You are an original, uniquely equipped for exactly this place and moment in time.

04
You are
a new creation.

> **Look to His Word:**

Therefore, if anyone is in Christ,
the new creation has come:
The old has gone, the new is here!

2 CORINTHIANS 5:17 (NIV)

See it for yourself:

When you gave your life to Christ, you became a new creation! You're not who you were. You have a different identity. You are now a son or daughter of the Most High God. You are holy, righteous, blameless, and honorable in His sight because of the sacrifice of His Son, Jesus, on your behalf. God doesn't see all the sin or bad you've done. He only sees the blood of Jesus washing you clean. Your mistakes or failures haven't canceled your destiny — God doesn't consult your past to determine your future. The enemy wants you to live in shame, fear, guilt, and confusion, but you are set free from your past. You can live in peace and victory because you are brand new!

05

You are
never alone.

> ### Look to His Word:

"I will never fail you.
I will never abandon you."

HEBREWS 13:5

See it for yourself:

You may feel alone or abandoned, but God is with you. You may be facing the toughest of battles or longest of trials, but God is with you. You are not forgotten. He is Emmanuel, "God with us." You can never escape from God or get away from His presence (Psalm 139:7). You are safe and secure in the palm of His hands. Always remember this truth. He sees you, and He will take care of you. He will also bring people into your life to support you and fight alongside you. In the midst of opposition and the negative voices of this world, do not grow weary or faint. You are not running the race of life alone. God is right by your side.

06 You are *free.*

Look to His Word:

"So if the Son sets you free, you are truly free."

JOHN 8:36

See it for yourself:

God didn't create us to be partially free or almost free. One version of John 8:36 says, *"If the Son sets you free from sin, then become a true son and be unquestionably free"* (TPT). The things that are keeping you bound and hindering your potential are not permanent. That is not how your story ends. We serve the God of the breakthrough, and where His Spirit lives, there is liberty. The memories or addictions or problems that plague you are not too big for God. You are far too valuable to Him, and your destiny is far too great for you to be drained of joy and restricted in growth. You are not a slave. You are free! God has healed you, renewed your mind, and broken every chain.

07 You are *loved.*

> Look to His Word:

"For this is how God loved the world: He gave his one and only Son, so that everyone who believes in him will not perish but have eternal life."

JOHN 3:16

See it for yourself:

Y ou are not defined by your mistakes, your past, your family, your zip code, or your performance. Rather, you are defined by God's amazing love for you. He loves you so much that He sent His Son to die for you. Jesus paid the price for every sin and wrong you've ever done because He wants to spend all of eternity with *you!* You are wanted, accepted, and pursued. Before you were even born, He had His eye on you. Be assured. His arms are wide open to you every day, waiting for you to run to Him. What moves God is not only your love for Him but when you recognize His love for you. It pleases God when you know you are dearly loved. So lift your head high and walk with confidence. You are deeply loved by your Creator.

08 You are secure in God's love.

Look to His Word:

And I am convinced that nothing can ever separate us from God's love. Neither death nor life, neither angels nor demons, neither our fears for today nor our worries about tomorrow — not even the powers of hell can separate us from God's love. No power in the sky above or in the earth below — indeed, nothing in all creation will ever be able to separate us from the love of God that is revealed in Christ Jesus our Lord.

ROMANS 8:38–39

See it for yourself:

No matter what you have been through or how you feel about yourself, God's love is unconditional and unchanging. Nothing, absolutely *nothing*, can separate you from it! Nor can anything cancel His love for you. You don't have to do anything special to make God love you. In other words, you don't have to do anything to earn it. You may face challenges in this life, but always remember that you are surrounded and pursued by His great, abounding, never-ending love. The world may shift and shake, but rest in the knowledge that God's love is unshakable, all-encompassing, and absolute. You are not too much for Him, and you don't ever have to worry about whether you are or not. He loves every part of you. You are completely secure and safe in His love. You are permanently loved.

09 You are *strong.*

> Look to His Word:

For I can do everything through Christ,
who gives me strength.

PHILIPPIANS 4:13

See it for yourself:

Y ou have already overcome many trials and obstacles in your life, not only physically but emotionally, mentally, and spiritually. Look back on all the things you have endured and conquered. You are still here. You are strong! What you're up against may seem intimidating or too big to handle, but as you face challenges, you are not on your own. Through Christ, you are able. You can find supernatural strength, power, and stamina in Him. God knows how much you're able to handle, and He will give you everything you need to handle it. Let *". . . the joy of the LORD [be] your strength"* (Nehemiah 8:10), and let His Spirit empower you. And even when you feel weak, you will always be able to bear whatever comes your way.

10 You are *a temple of the Holy Spirit.*

Look to His Word:

Don't you realize that your body is the temple of the Holy Spirit, who lives in you and was given to you by God? . . .

1 CORINTHIANS 6:19

See it for yourself:

Your body is a temple of the Most High God, a vessel in which He dwells. You belong to Him. That means sickness, addiction, immorality — any negative thing — does not have a place in your body. Declare today that you are a temple of the Holy Spirit and that you were created to be whole, healthy, and blessed. Rebuke that illness or addiction in Jesus' name. Resist the enemy's temptations. You are filled with the Spirit of God . . . so represent Him to this world. When you take care of your body — when you make an effort to present yourself as excellent — and honor your whole body as His temple, you honor God. He created you as a holy temple to hold His presence. Act like it.

11 You are *chosen.*

Look to His Word:

"You didn't choose me. I chose you. . . ."

JOHN 15:16

See it for yourself:

You are not a by-product of fate. You are not here by chance or coincidence; you're here on purpose! You are handpicked, approved, and *chosen*. Let that truth sink in and shift your perspective today. You may think you don't measure up or don't deserve His love or have too many flaws, but none of that stops God. That doesn't disqualify you. In His great mercy and love, God has still chosen you and anointed you. Think of all the unlikely people God chose in the Bible to do great things — Moses, David, Peter, Mary . . . . With God on your side, you will go further than people who may have more talent or resources. He knows your potential, and He's already given you what you need to fulfill your assignment. You are a perfect fit.

You are
both valuable and worthy.

12

> ### Look to His Word:

"So don't be afraid; you are more valuable to God than a whole flock of sparrows."

MATTHEW 10:31

See it for yourself:

Your worth doesn't come from people or things or something you've done. It comes from God alone — the One who spoke the universe into being and breathed life into your body. You are a child of the Most High God, made worthy by what Jesus did, and only He can place value upon your life. Don't let someone else make you feel like you don't deserve certain things. The enemy cannot determine your worth. Your performance doesn't determine who you are. In fact, there's nothing anyone can say or anything you can do that will change your worth in His eyes. Tune out the enemy's lies and receive the truth today. You are worthy. You are created in God's image and blessed with His favor. Let the insecurity and inferiority roll off you. You are more valuable to Him than anything else in all creation.

13 You are *God's masterpiece.*

Look to His Word:

For we are God's masterpiece. He has created us anew in Christ Jesus, so we can do the good things he planned for us long ago.

EPHESIANS 2:10

See it for yourself:

You are intricately designed, created by a good God. Don't let the opinions of others tell you who you are or try to belittle your value. You are not an accident or a mishap. God did not say, "Whoops!" when you were born. He stepped back and said, "That is very good." You have been painted by the most incredible artist in existence, and He signed His name on you: Made by Almighty God. You may feel broken or damaged or unworthy, but that's not how God sees you. You are God's very own masterpiece, designed with purpose and potential! You have special gifts and talents that are meant to shine, and you have a great destiny ahead of you.

14 You are *precious.*

Look to His Word:

"Others were given in exchange for you. I traded their lives for yours because you are precious to me. You are honored, and I love you."

ISAIAH 43:4

See it for yourself:

You are a beloved child of the Most High God. You are precious in His sight — of great value and held with great care by the King of Kings. Don't let anyone make you feel inferior or forgotten or unworthy. Don't focus on your flaws, limitations, or disappointments as indicators of your worth. Your environment doesn't change your identity. Gold is still gold no matter where it is. Decide today what you're choosing to dwell on. You were formed by God with purpose, and He doesn't make mistakes. Jesus Christ, who knew no sin, traded His life for yours on a cross, and you can come boldly to His throne. Your life is of incalculable worth to the Father — beyond that of all the gold and gems of the earth. You are exquisite, priceless, beloved. You are precious.

15 You are empowered.

Look to His Word:

"But you will receive power when the Holy Spirit comes upon you. And you will be my witnesses, telling people about me everywhere — in Jerusalem, throughout Judea, in Samaria, and to the ends of the earth."

ACTS 1:8

See it for yourself:

The enemy wants you to feel weak, defeated, lacking, less than. But that is not how you were created to operate. God has empowered you with His very Spirit. That makes you very powerful. The challenges you face may be huge, but they're no match for our God! The same power that raised Christ from the dead, split the Red Sea, and opened prison doors lives in you (Romans 8:11). You are being given the power to bring dead things to life, create a new legacy for your family, break through sickness and dysfunction, and tell the world about the power of our God. There is a force backing you that's greater than any force trying to stop you. Begin to see yourself as you truly are: empowered to do all God has called you to do.

16 You are a friend of God.

Look to His Word:

"I no longer call you servants, because a servant does not know his master's business. Instead, I have called you friends, for everything that I learned from my Father I have made known to you."

JOHN 15:15 (NIV)

See it for yourself:

The God of the universe calls you friend! This is not only a title — it's an invitation into a personal relationship with Him. This means you can approach Him confidently with your dreams, your struggles, and your joys, just like you would a good friend. His face lights up, and He smiles when you come to Him. He loves spending time with you, hearing your concerns and what you're dreaming about. He is always there, ready to listen and guide you. He understands what you're walking through and doesn't hold your mistakes against you. You are not a servant or a stranger or a distant relation. You are not out of sight, out of mind. He is always thinking of you and will never leave you. You are His friend.

17
You are an heir with Christ.

Look to His Word:

And since we are his children, we are his heirs. In fact, together with Christ we are heirs of God's glory.

ROMANS 8:17

See it for yourself:

When Jesus died and rose again, He made a way for all people to come to Him, both Jews and Gentiles. Galatians 3:29 (NKJV) says, *"And if you are Christ's, then you are Abraham's seed, and heirs according to the promise."* Everything that belongs to Christ also belongs to you. Together with Jesus, you share an inheritance of favor, victory, and blessing. Your legacy is glory. That doesn't mean you won't experience trouble or hardship in this life, because you will, but be assured that Jesus has overcome the world (John 16:33). Your strife and your difficulties are not going to last forever. You are an heir of the King and a co-heir with Jesus Christ! Goodness and mercy are following you. Abundance, love, victory, and freedom are your promised inheritance.

18

You are *a child of God and have been adopted into God's family.*

Look to His Word:

See how very much our Father loves us, for he calls us his children, and that is what we are! . . .

1 JOHN 3:1

See it for yourself:

You have been adopted into the chosen family of God! That makes you His beloved child — protected, valued, and deeply loved. It doesn't matter what is happening in your earthly family or what your natural heritage or DNA says; when you accept Christ, you are born into a new family and receive a new spiritual birth certificate. It says you're a son or daughter of the Most High God. He is not only all-powerful and all-knowing — He is your Father. And with adoption comes all the benefits of sonship. The enemy knows who you are and will try to feed you lies. But you belong to God, adopted and fully accepted into His family. So rebuke the enemy and carry yourself like a king, like a queen, like a child of the Most High.

19

You are God's favorite.

Look to His Word:

But anyone who does not love does not know God, for God is love. God showed how much he loved us by sending his one and only Son into the world so that we might have eternal life through him.

1 JOHN 4:8-9

See it for yourself:

If God had a cell phone, you would be in His favorite contacts. You've probably heard that God doesn't have favorites. But His love is unlimited. Just because one person is given His love doesn't mean someone else gets less. And He doesn't just display love — He *is* love. It's who He is. Begin calling yourself His favorite. Go to Him with boldness, pray daring prayers, ask Him for your dreams, believe for your finances or health or family to turn around, and expect opportunities to come your way. Not because of who you are or because you've earned it but because of who your Father is. You are His favorite, and He will move Heaven and the earth to be good to you.

You are redeemed.

Look to His Word:

In him we have redemption through his blood, the forgiveness of sins, in accordance with the riches of God's grace.

EPHESIANS 1:7 (NIV)

See it for yourself:

Being a believer doesn't guarantee you won't be hurt, disappointed, or experience delays, but you won't have to live defeated, resentful, and bitter as a result. God knows how to redeem everything you've been through. Through the blood of Jesus, you have redemption and the forgiveness of sin. It's not because of something you've done or earned; it's because of His great love and grace. He will restore the years lost and the things stolen (Joel 2:25–27). God will turn every evil thing set against you into good. He is in control, and He will work things out. He will open new doors, bring new opportunities, and restore you with kindness. You can trust Him to redeem it all.

21
You are *more than a conqueror.*

Look to His Word:

Yet in all these things we are more than conquerors through Him who loved us.

ROMANS 8:37 (NKJV)

See it for yourself:

Nothing in your life is too much for you to handle. We all go through challenges, disappointments, hurts, and unfair situations, and it's easy to throw a pity party or give up. But God has promised that through Him, we are more than conquerors. The same Spirit that raised Christ from the dead lives in you, and He will gift you with the wisdom, strength, and energy you need to rise above any circumstance and see victory. Don't entertain defeat. Whether you're experiencing a minor problem or facing a major disappointment, keep a victor mentality. God is sovereign, and you will triumph over the enemy by the blood of the Lamb and the word of your testimony (Revelation 12:11). You are not a victim. You are a conqueror.

22

You are *kept safe.*

Look to His Word:

. . . His faithful promises are your armor and protection.

PSALM 91:4

See it for yourself:

God is your defender. Every battle belongs to Him, and He has never lost. He wants you to know that you are safe with Him. His promises are your armor. Your reputation is safe with Him. Your family is safe with Him. Your finances are safe with Him. Your health is safe with Him. You do not have to fear trouble or calamity — you are covered by the blood of Jesus and kept hidden from harm. You are in a safe place. You do not need to worry or feel anxious because He is strong and able and by your side through every trial. He knows how to distract your enemies and give you shelter in the storm. When you trust in Him, He has victory and provision in store for you. Let Him fight your battles as you rest in Him.

23

You are *blessed with every spiritual blessing.*

Look to His Word:

All praise to God, the Father of our Lord Jesus Christ, who has blessed us with every spiritual blessing in the heavenly realms because we are united with Christ.

EPHESIANS 1:3

See it for yourself:

The enemy will try to say, "You don't deserve to be blessed. Look at the mistakes you've made or the family you've come from. You don't measure up." Shake off his lies. Because of Jesus, you are made new. You are a son or daughter of God, and you have been given all the benefits and spiritual blessings of being so. You have full access to God's wisdom, peace, love, provision, strength, and grace. You are given the fruits of the Spirit. You are given spiritual gifts that can impact the world. You are spiritually enriched, and your cup overflows. This is not because of something you have done or earned — it's because of Christ. You can simply believe and receive from Him today.

You are the head — not the tail.

Look to His Word:

The LORD will make you the head, not the tail. If you pay attention to the commands of the LORD your God that I give you this day and carefully follow them, you will always be at the top, never at the bottom.

DEUTERONOMY 28:13 (NIV)

See it for yourself:

When you honor God and keep Him in first place, what limits others won't limit you. He hides you from the enemy, and you come out on top. You will see overflow and abundance, blessings running over. You will have favor and provision. You will not be left behind. Even in famine, in a down economy, in an inhospitable environment, God is your source, and as you follow Him, He will make you the head and not the tail. You are ahead and not behind. Quit living out of fear, and start living out of faith. You are blessed when you come in and blessed when you go out (Deuteronomy 28:6). Your Father is a good God, and He takes pleasure in prospering you.

25

You are
a significant part of the body of Christ.

Look to His Word:

Just as our bodies have many parts and each part has a special function, so it is with Christ's body. We are many parts of one body, and we all belong to each other.

ROMANS 12:4–5

See it for yourself:

You are not exempt from the Church or from being part of the body of Christ. It doesn't matter who you were in the past or what kind of family you originated from; because of Christ's work on the cross, you are now part of His Church. First Corinthians 12:27 says, *"All of you together are Christ's body, and each of you is a part of it."* You belong. You are not an outlier or an outcast, and you have a significant part to play. Just like how a body cannot function without every part working together, you have specific gifts and talents given to you by God that are needed to serve and help build His Kingdom. God has placed you in His Church for a reason and a purpose. You are vital. You are important.

26

You are *a royal priesthood.*

Look to His Word:

. . . for you are a chosen people. You are royal priests, a holy nation, God's very own possession. As a result, you can show others the goodness of God, for he called you out of the darkness into his wonderful light.

1 PETER 2:9

See it for yourself:

You have been grafted into a royal bloodline — set apart to serve God and show others His love. Your DNA is special. God has called you chosen, priestly, and holy — His special possession. Your natural bloodline may be filled with impurities or problems, addictions and mistakes, but your spiritual bloodline is royal, pure, and powerful. And the spiritual is always greater than the natural. You have been marked by Almighty God to minister to Him and to those around you. It doesn't matter what other people say about you or what you look like. Through Christ, you are a royal priest. Your spiritual lineage is strong and victorious, and you are called to stand tall and walk with purpose, influence, and dignity.

27 You are *healed.*

Look to His Word:

He personally carried our sins in his body on the cross so that we can be dead to sin and live for what is right. By his wounds you are healed.

1 PETER 2:24

See it for yourself:

God made your body. He knows all its inner workings. There is nothing He cannot restore or heal, and He has the supernatural power to do the impossible. Don't believe the enemy's lies about your body. Don't let worry or anxiety drain you. Don't claim that sickness as your own. God is Jehovah Rapha, the Lord our Healer. Jesus "... *carried our sorrows ... [and] was wounded for our transgressions ... [but] by His stripes we are healed*" (Isaiah 53:4–5, NKJV). The price has been paid for your healing. It is part of your inheritance as a follower of Christ. God is far greater than any sickness, disease, or addiction that's coming against you. Those things are no match for you. Believe in your healing, receive it, and thank God for it. Jehovah Rapha has the final word.

28

You are *a citizen of Heaven.*

Look to His Word:

But we are citizens of heaven, where the Lord Jesus Christ lives. And we are eagerly waiting for him to return as our Savior.

PHILIPPIANS 3:20

See it for yourself:

You are part of this world, but it is not your home. You are a citizen of a divine, Heavenly realm. That is your identity, your heritage, your home. God has rescued you from the kingdom of darkness and brought you to a Kingdom of light (Colossians 1:13). The heroes of the faith and a great cloud of witnesses who have gone before you are cheering you on from Heaven as you run your race (Hebrews 12:1). So keep your eyes on eternal things. Focus on God's truths, love, and promises. Don't become caught up in current trends or blinded by worries. The circumstances of your current life are fleeting and temporary. Your true, eternal home is with the Most High God.

29

You are
provided for.

Look to His Word:

And my God will meet all your needs according to the riches of his glory in Christ Jesus.

PHILIPPIANS 4:19 (NIV)

See it for yourself:

Our God owns it all. He holds wealth beyond measure. He can make streams in the desert and streets out of gold. And you are His child. He wants to provide for you. He wants to meet all your needs. He has already lined up the right people to open doors for you. He has orchestrated the big break, the job offer, the miraculous check in the mail. He wants to open the windows of Heaven and bring overflowing blessing into your life. He's already placed provision in your future — not only financially but emotionally, socially, and physically. You do not have to fear. You are not at a deficit. Even in famine, in trouble, in the fiery furnace of trials, the righteous have more than enough (Psalm 37:19). It gives God pleasure to bless you, so you can testify to His goodness and then are able to turn around to bless others.

You are
a servant.

30

> *Look to His Word:*

"... Whoever wants to be a leader among you must be your servant, and whoever wants to be first among you must be the slave of everyone else. For even the Son of Man came not to be served but to serve others and to give his life as a ransom for many."

MARK 10:43–45

See it for yourself:

Jesus said if you want to be a leader, you have to serve people. This isn't a thing you do every so often, nor is it something that's forced upon you. Jesus was talking about a willing lifestyle defined by continuously looking for ways to serve God and help others. This is something that becomes part of who you are — being a servant of God's will and a servant of others. Don't become too distracted with life that you forget who God has called you to be. You are never too big, too influential, too busy, or too high up in the business or perhaps your church to serve someone else. Jesus Himself washed feet. Walk in humility as a servant of the Most High God and care for people, and you will be graciously welcomed into the Kingdom.

＃ You are a partaker of the divine nature.

Look to His Word:

And because of his glory and excellence,
he has given us great and precious promises.
These are the promises that enable you to
share his divine nature and escape the world's
corruption caused by human desires.

2 PETER 1:4

See it for yourself:

When you gave your life to Christ, you were invited into a divine relationship with the Creator of the universe and given great promises. You are no longer bound by your human frailty or weakness or sin. You can share in and reflect the qualities of the Almighty God in your daily life. Because of Christ, you are transformed in His likeness. You are able to rise above your limitations and mirror the character of God. You have a new divine identity — one filled with love, kindness, grace, hope, humility, and compassion — and you are actively participating in something greater than yourself. Your life is intertwined with Christ. You are partaking in the divine nature of our holy God.

32

You are
a witness.

Look to His Word:

"But you will receive power when the Holy Spirit comes upon you. And you will be my witnesses . . ."

ACTS 1:8

See it for yourself:

Scripture says we receive power to be His witnesses. It doesn't say "to witness" nor does it say to preach a sermon, straighten people out, or tell them what they're doing wrong. No, the real power is to be a witness. Your life is the message. The transformation from who you were to who you are in Christ is a significant testimony of God's great love and miracle-working power. Do not look down on your story or think your life won't influence others. As the Holy Spirit empowers you, share your life with others. You don't have to give a sermon or pass out pamphlets. The story of your life can offer comfort and give people a glimpse of God's love and truth all on its own.

33

You are *justified.*

Look to His Word:

Therefore, having been justified by faith, we have peace with God through our Lord Jesus Christ.

ROMANS 5:1 (NKJV)

See it for yourself:

We are all sinners. We have all fallen short of God's glory and perfection (Romans 3:23–24). But God is holy, completely sinless, and we could not have full access to Him or an eternity in Heaven without Jesus' sacrifice on the cross. Christ's blood made a way for us to be made right with God. You can approach God boldly and with peace because you have been justified through your faith in Jesus. You are vindicated. It's not by your works but by your belief in Him as the Son of God who died for your sins and rose again in power. Despite your imperfections, your flaws, and your sins, you are reconciled to and accepted by the God of the universe. Give thanks today that you have been given access now and forever to the Most High God!

34

You are *making a difference.*

Look to His Word:

Let us not become weary in doing good,
for at the proper time we will reap a harvest
if we do not give up.

GALATIANS 6:9 (NIV)

See it for yourself:

You were created to make a difference in the world. God has a specific assignment that only you can accomplish, specific people only you can help, and specific tasks only you have the gifts to tackle. It may not seem like it some days, but people need you. Your presence in the room matters. Your laughter and encouragement and high fives matter. The words you say matter. Do not grow weary if you don't see a great response from your hard work, if no one calls you to say thanks, or if no one acknowledges what you did. God sees it all, and one day, if you don't give up, you will reap a harvest for God's Kingdom. Every good thing you do for the people around you makes a difference.

35

You are *being sanctified.*

Look to His Word:

... But you were washed, but you were sanctified, but you were justified in the name of the Lord Jesus and by the Spirit of our God.

1 CORINTHIANS 6:11 (NKJV)

See it for yourself:

Y ou are saved and justified, and God has a great destiny in store for you, but becoming holy and set apart is a journey. God is always dealing with us about something. He always wants us to go to a new level. To do that, we need to say no to our flesh over and over. We need to take up our cross *daily* (Luke 9:23). Sanctification is a continuous process. You may have days when resisting temptation is difficult or you falter in moving forward with Christ, but don't let the enemy condemn you for not having everything together yet. God doesn't require you to be perfect; there is grace as you walk on the path of being sanctified. As you ask Him to search your heart and take steps to be more like Him, you will be transformed.

You are an ambassador for Christ.

Look to His Word:

So we are Christ's ambassadors; God is making his appeal through us. We speak for Christ when we plead, "Come back to God!"

2 CORINTHIANS 5:20

See it for yourself:

An ambassador is a person who represents or advocates for someone or something else, and Scripture says we are exactly this — God's representatives on this earth. People can't see God, but they can see you. With every one of your words and actions, you represent God to a lost and dying world. You have the responsibility and honor of carrying the Good News of Jesus Christ into your community, your work, and your home. Represent Him with joy and a smile! You have God's truth to offer a world that needs guidance. And when you live out your faith in an authentic and genuine way, you show others the great love and joy of the Most High God. Everywhere you go and with everything you do, be reminded today of your impact. Your role as an ambassador is vital for the Kingdom of God.

37

You are
cared for.

> **Look to His Word:**

Cast all your anxiety on him because he cares for you.

1 PETER 5:7 (NIV)

See it for yourself:

God has never failed His people. Nothing can defeat Him or stop what He has planned for your life. The Most High God is by your side always. He will fight your battles. He will give you wisdom. He will make a way where you don't see one. He will take care of the details. Cast all your anxieties, worries, and fears at His feet today. Jesus says, *"And if God cares so wonderfully for wildflowers that are here today and thrown into the fire tomorrow, he will certainly care for you . . ."* (Matthew 6:30). You are so much more valuable to Him than wildflowers, and He knows what you need better than you do. Trust in His great sovereignty and love for you, and He will bring you peace. You are loved beyond measure.

You are blessed to be a blessing.

Look to His Word:

If you keep yourself pure, you will be a special utensil for honorable use. Your life will be clean, and you will be ready for the Master to use you for every good work.

2 TIMOTHY 2:21

See it for yourself:

Proverbs says that a good person leaves an inheritance for their children's children (Proverbs 13:22). You aren't blessed simply for your own gain. You're blessed so you can leave an inheritance, so that you lend and not borrow, share with others, and build God's Kingdom even further. When you are blessed with knowledge, it's so you can use it to help others. When you are blessed with finances, it's so you can be generous toward those in need. When you are blessed with provision, it's so you can provide for your family now and in the future. When you are blessed with creativity and ingenuity, it's so you can create lifesaving products and inventions for others. You are blessed so that you can be a special instrument used for every good work — so you can be a blessing to others. You are blessed to leave a legacy.

You are
a branch of the vine.

Look to His Word:

"I am the vine; you are the branches. If you remain in me and I in you, you will bear much fruit; apart from me you can do nothing."

JOHN 15:5 (NIV)

See it for yourself:

There's always something in life we feel we have to fix, improve upon, gain approval for, or do better in, but we weren't created to live like that. Psalm 46:10 says, *"Be still, and know that I am God. . . ."* You don't have to make everything happen for yourself. You don't have to fix everything. Relieve the pressure and focus instead on abiding with God. You are a branch connected to a fruitful vine, and as you remain in Christ, God will do the rest. Scripture says: *"Seek the Kingdom of God above all else, and live righteously, and he will give you everything you need"* (Matthew 6:33). Turn every situation over to God, do your best with what you have, and then rest in God's peace. You are a branch. Abide in Him as your source, and you will have everything you need and bear much fruit.

You are covered by God's grace.

Look to His Word:

God saved you by his grace when you believed. And you can't take credit for this; it is a gift from God.

EPHESIANS 2:8

See it for yourself:

So many people think that God is only interested in offering grace to the "good people" — the ones who have it all together and hardly ever make mistakes. But our God is not like that. When you mess up, He doesn't turn away from you; He turns toward you. His grace comes looking for you. You can always expect Him to have grace, compassion, goodness, and love for you. No mistake is too much for the mercy of God. He is not angry at you. He is head-over-heels in love with you, and because of Christ's sacrifice, His grace completely covers your past, present, and future. You may not deserve it, and you can do nothing to earn it, but it's there for you as a free gift, just waiting for you to receive it. Shake off the guilt and condemnation today and hold your head high. Grace is available to you.

You are *made in the image of God.*

Look to His Word:

So God created mankind in his own image,
in the image of God he created them;
male and female he created them.

GENESIS 1:27 (NIV)

See it for yourself:

You are wonderfully made (Psalm 139:14) because you were created in the image of a wonderful God! You are His child — so don't entertain the idea of any other picture of yourself. Don't let the enemy's words or labels fill your heart. Give God control of your self-image — not the media, not your family, not your job, not a tragedy, and certainly not the enemy. The only One who can show you who you truly are is the One who made you. Let His Word define you; it says you are made in His image to resemble Him. He created you with His DNA — you have royal blood flowing in your veins — and He breathed His life into you. You display God's nature and character to a lost, lonely, and hurting world. Don't discount who you are.

You are able to hear God's voice.

Look to His Word:

"My sheep hear My voice, and I know them, and they follow Me."

JOHN 10:27 (NKJV)

See it for yourself:

We all have physical ears, but we also have spiritual ears. God is constantly speaking to His people, and He wants you to know that you have the ability to hear Him. He may not talk to you like other people do; it may not be dramatic or loud. In Scripture, God spoke to many people in different ways — through dreams, visions, a sense in their spirit, or a still small voice. He may put ideas or thoughts in your spirit as a seed that He wants to grow. Learn to listen to His promptings. Ask Him to help open your spiritual ears and discern His voice from all the others vying for your attention. And when you do hear Him, check what you've heard against God's written Word. Obey what He says, and then believe with all your heart that you will see what you've heard.

You are
an overcomer of fear.

Look to His Word:

I sought the LORD, and he answered me;
he delivered me from all my fears.

PSALM 34:4 (NIV)

See it for yourself:

The world is filled with reasons to be afraid. God knew there would be some shadowy days, some dark valleys, some troubled times, but He doesn't leave us alone to conquer it. David said of God, *"Even when I walk through the darkest valley, I will not be afraid, for you are close beside me . . ."* (Psalm 23:4). Shift your heart from fear to faith, from panic to peace. Your God is greater, stronger, and more powerful than anything that can come against you. He is on your side, fighting your battles, and watching over you. He is your shield and shepherd. The next time fear knocks, answer with faith! *"The LORD is my light and my salvation; whom shall I fear? . . ."* (Psalm 27:1, NKJV). Refuse to let fear, worry, or anxiety keep you from your destiny. Through Christ, you have overcome. You have victory over the spirit of fear.

You are victorious.

Look to His Word:

For everyone born of God overcomes the world. This is the victory that has overcome the world, even our faith.

1 JOHN 5:4 (NIV)

See it for yourself:

You are not a victim. You are not a loser. You are not defeated. You are *victorious*. Start talking to yourself like the winner God made you to be. Your inheritance, as a son or daughter of the Most High God, is victory. All the odds may be against you, and you may have lost some ground, but God will win the war. Because with God on your side, the odds dramatically change. He gives you the victory through Christ (1 Corinthians 15:57). And if you stay in agreement with God, He will take what is meant for evil and use it for good. That difficulty won't defeat you. That illness won't defeat you. That loss won't defeat you. God will use everything to your advantage and your good (Romans 8:28). You may not understand how, but He does. Through Him, you have victory.

You are anointed.

Look to His Word:

As for you, the anointing you received from him remains in you, and you do not need anyone to teach you. But as his anointing teaches you about all things and as that anointing is real, not counterfeit — just as it has taught you, remain in him.

1 JOHN 2:27 (NIV)

See it for yourself:

The Most High God has anointed you. That means He has put a power in you — a power that cannot be dimmed or defeated. It's a power that will make up for anything you don't have and will teach you about all things. You don't determine how high or how far you're going to go. That is determined by the Almighty God breathing on your life. And when you think you can't go any further or things won't work out, speak out in faith and step into the anointing God has given you. Then watch as you are set free and healed. You are empowered to overcome because of God's anointing on your life and *". . . because the Spirit who lives in you is greater than the spirit who lives in the world"* (1 John 4:4).

You are here for such a time as this.

Look to His Word:

"... And who knows but that you have come to your royal position for such a time as this?"

ESTHER 4:14 (NIV)

See it for yourself:

God has orchestrated you to be born at this exact moment in time to your exact parents in your exact location. He matched you perfectly for your world. You are not out of place. You're not in the wrong neighborhood. You have the right personality. You're the right nationality. You have the right gifts and talents. God has ordained everything about you and has already planned out your days. He placed in you exactly what you need to fulfill His plan for your life. When the right time comes, you will finally understand. It will all make sense. You will discover both the abilities and the potential that perhaps you never knew you had. You will see His plan come to life. You are not here by accident. God chose you to be here, in this generation, at this precise time in history.

You are
a recipient of God's compassion.

47

Look to His Word:

Praise be to the God and Father of our Lord Jesus Christ, the Father of compassion and the God of all comfort.

2 CORINTHIANS 1:3 (NIV)

See it for yourself:

God doesn't ever look at you with disdain or contempt. He doesn't turn a blind eye when you experience hardship or trouble. Like a good Father, He is compassionate when you experience difficulties or when you're struggling with your sense of self. You can run to Him with all of your problems and pains. Even when you do something wrong or make a big mess, you can always turn to Him for help. He is there with His arms wide open, ready to treat you with patience and kindness. He wants to comfort you and dry your tears. He dearly loves you, and you will always receive sympathy and care from Him. He continuously looks upon you, His beloved child, with compassion in His heart.

You are *given a future filled with hope.*

Look to His Word:

"For I know the plans I have for you," declares the Lord, "plans to prosper you and not to harm you, plans to give you hope and a future."

JEREMIAH 29:11 (NIV)

See it for yourself:

You are not at the mercy of fate, happenstance, or coincidence. You don't have to say, "I hope this works out." You can be confident that God is ordering your steps and upholding you with His hand (Psalm 37:23–24). You can live in peace, knowing everything is not just up to you. God has gone ahead of you. He is on the throne, and He is in control. Even if your present moment is confusing and filled with disappointment or obstacles that feel too big, there is something happening behind the scenes. God is working, making paths for you. God has some things in your future that are going to boggle your mind — He has been orchestrating it all for you. What looks like a setback in your present may very well be a setup for your destiny. Your future is filled with good things.

49

You are *pure.*

> ### Look to His Word:

But if we walk in the light, as he is in the light, we have fellowship with one another, and the blood of Jesus, his Son, purifies us from all sin.

1 JOHN 1:7 (NIV)

See it for yourself:

Y ou are not dirty, filthy, or unclean. You may have things in your past that make you feel that way, but through Christ, you have been set free. You have been washed as white as snow. You have been covered by the blood of Jesus and purified from all sin. You are unblemished. You are pure. The stain of sin has been washed away. People may call you names or try to make you feel unclean, but God knows everything about you and still doesn't see your sin or shame. He only sees His purified son or daughter, and through His power, you can live a new life of purity in your mind and body. Seek to keep your heart pure before Him, and He will bless you (Matthew 5:8).

You are
equipped for every good work.

Look to His Word:

So that the servant of God may be thoroughly equipped for every good work.

2 TIMOTHY 3:17 (NIV)

See it for yourself:

God will never give you an assignment and not provide you with what you need to do it successfully. You are not lacking. You are not operating out of scarcity. You're not the back-up plan. You are *thoroughly* equipped and empowered through Christ. Don't let the enemy tell you otherwise. Doubt cannot stay, insecurity has to leave, and worry must be evicted. If there is something God is telling you to do, do not second guess your ability to do it simply because you gave place to the wrong things in your mind and spirit. Let God's words about yourself guide you. Let His power give you strength, wisdom, guidance, peace, and knowledge to do all He has called you to do.

But God shows his love for us in *that while we were still sinners,* Christ died for us.

ROMANS 5:8 (ESV)

51

You are *covered by God's wings and are shielded from the enemy.*

Look to His Word:

For he will conceal me there when troubles come; he will hide me in his sanctuary. He will place me out of reach on a high rock.

PSALM 27:5

See it for yourself:

The enemy wants to keep you from your destiny, and many things may be sent to stop you: trouble, bad breaks, catastrophe, sickness. But when you make the Lord your God, when you stay under the shelter of the Most High, He will cover you with His wings (Psalm 91:4). Difficulties will come, but they will not end your story. He will place you out of reach. He will hide you where you cannot be found. He will make you invisible to people and circumstances designed to harm you. Like the Israelites who put the blood of a lamb on their doorposts so the death angel would pass over their homes, you are hidden from the enemy because of the blood of Christ. You don't have to live worried, fearing what might happen. Live in peace under the shelter of God's wings. He has the final say.

You are *a part of the new covenant.*

52

Look to His Word:

"This is the covenant I will establish with the people of Israel after that time, declares the Lord. I will put my laws in their minds and write them on their hearts. I will be their God, and they will be my people."

HEBREWS 8:10 (NIV)

See it for yourself:

In the Old Testament, priests had to go to the temple to make sacrifices for the people's sins. That's how they earned forgiveness. They lived under constant pressure. There were hundreds of rules to follow, and their work was never done. Another sacrifice was always required. But when Jesus was crucified, He said, *"It is finished"* (John 19:30, NIV). And the Scripture says Jesus now sits at the right hand of the Father (Hebrews 1:3). Under the new covenant, Jesus is sitting down at rest because it is done — there are no more sacrifices for forgiveness, no more pressure. The price has been paid for humanity's sins, and Christ has already defeated every enemy. You are part of this new covenant. You are not working to get the victory. You are working *from* victory. Now you can live from a place of rest, peace, and trust.

You are
a recipient of eternal life.

53

Look to His Word:

"Very truly I tell you, whoever hears my word and believes him who sent me has eternal life and will not be judged but has crossed over from death to life."

JOHN 5:24 (NIV)

See it for yourself:

You have crossed over from death to life. Scripture says in John 3:16, *"For this is how God loved the world: He gave his one and only Son, so that everyone who believes in him will not perish but have eternal life."* When you repented your sin and gave your heart to Jesus, your name was written in the Lamb's Book of Life. You were saved! Through your faith in Him and God's immeasurable grace, your present life on this earth is transformed, and your eternity in His presence is assured. Eternal life with Jesus is the greatest gift you will ever receive. Don't let the enemy tell you lies about your future. Don't doubt God's love or the truth of His Word. With faith in Jesus, you are given eternal life.

You are given a spirit of power, love, and self-discipline.

Look to His Word:

For God has not given us a spirit of fear and timidity, but of power, love, and self-discipline.

2 TIMOTHY 1:7

See it for yourself:

There is a war going on inside all of us between our flesh and our spirit, between giving in to our carnal nature and self-control, between what we feel in the moment and what we know for eternity. The enemy wants you to give in to your impulses of fear, hatred, and indulgence, but Scripture says, *"A person without self-control is like a city with broken-down walls"* (Proverbs 25:28). If you keep sowing to the flesh, you'll reap defeat. But if you'll start sowing to the Spirit, you'll reap victory. God has given you the strength to live without being ruled by your carnal desires. He has given you power, love, and self-discipline. Through Christ, you can say no to your flesh. As your spirit grows stronger, your flesh will get weaker, and you will step into the fullness of who God has called you to be.

55

You are not late.

> ### Look to His Word:
>
> There is a time for everything, and a season for every activity under the heavens.
>
> **ECCLESIASTES 3:1 (NIV)**

See it for yourself:

Everything that happens on this earth happens in God's time, and His timing is perfect. Quit comparing your story to someone else's. Stop comparing your timeline to someone else's. You are not too late, you are not behind, and you are not forgotten. You have not missed your chance. God didn't miscalculate the timing of your life. God is faithful, and your time will come. His promises are on their way. You may not see any sign of it, but God is working behind the scenes. Don't be discouraged. You are in a prime position for God to show off in your life. He wouldn't have promised what He did if He wasn't going to do it. Wait on the Lord and travel steadily on the path He has given you, and when the time is right, He will make it happen (Isaiah 60:22).

You are
promised peace of mind.

Look to His Word:

You will keep in perfect peace those whose minds are steadfast, because they trust in you.

ISAIAH 26:3 (NIV)

See it for yourself:

A mind at peace knows that God is in control. A mind at peace is not focused on problems; it's focused on promises. A mind at peace is not looking at how big the challenge is but how big our God is. God didn't create you to live anxiety-ridden, troubled, and on edge. That is from the enemy of your soul. God created you to live with peace through trust in Him. You can't stop the negative thoughts from coming, but you can decide whether or not you will dwell on them. You can instead decide to trust in God's sovereignty and goodness — on all the good things He says about you — and dismiss any confusion, fear, or doubt. You can take all the negative thoughts captive and evict them. Then God's perfect, supernatural peace that *". . . transcends all understanding . . ."* (Philippians 4:7, NIV) will set your heart and mind at ease.

You are
complete in Christ.

Look to His Word:

And in Christ you have been brought to fullness. He is the head over every power and authority.

COLOSSIANS 2:10 (NIV)

See it for yourself:

Life may have brought you trouble, and you may feel damaged or broken, but when you remain in Christ, every nook and cranny of your life is filled in with His love. Your heart is whole. That doesn't mean you won't have things to work on. You are still a work in progress, and you may still have struggles, weaknesses, and difficulties to navigate, but your eternal soul is full and complete. Through Him, you are given everlasting life and fully equipped with everything you need to grow and live out the destiny He's planned for you on this earth. In Him, you are complete and secure — there is nothing else you need to do or strive for to achieve standing with Him. He is above all and provides all, and you don't need to ever seek fulfilment elsewhere.

58

You are *heard.*

Look to His Word:

And we are confident that he hears us whenever we ask for anything that pleases him.

1 JOHN 5:14

See it for yourself:

When you pray, your prayers aren't hitting the ceiling or going into nothing in the atmosphere. Your prayers are going straight to the Father! He inclines His ear toward you. He hears every word you say, every prayer you mutter under your breath, and even the things you don't dare say out loud. You may feel like your prayers haven't been doing much or perhaps you've been waiting so long you think God doesn't care, but keep praying. The Scripture says He hears you, He loves you, and He is pleased to give you anything you ask within His will and in His name. Keep asking, and be confident in your prayers. Dare to pray God-sized prayers for all the things He's promised in His Word — supernatural favor, blessing, healing, peace, provision, and more — and He will show up in a big way.

59

You are
highly favored.

> *Look to His Word:*

Surely, LORD, you bless the righteous; you surround them with your favor . . .

PSALM 5:12 (NIV)

See it for yourself:

Everywhere you go and in everything you do, you have a benefit. You have a supernatural enabling upon your life that brings opportunities and causes the boundaries of your life to fall in pleasant places (Psalm 16:5). Shake off the doubt and discouragement. You may not see a way through your circumstances, but you can know with assurance that God will make a way. Begin to ask big, believe big, and walk with confidence. And as you live with bold expectancy, you'll see God take you places you've never been. He will make a way where there seems to be no way. He will give you impossible dreams, big breaks, healing, and freedom. You don't have ordinary or average favor on your life; you have extraordinary favor upon your life from the Most High God.

You are
surrounded by God's goodness.

> **Look to His Word:**

Surely your goodness and unfailing love will pursue me all the days of my life . . .

PSALM 23:6

See it for yourself:

God has been orchestrating things behind the scenes of your life to get you to where you are — people, promotions, protection, opportunities. His goodness and love have been chasing after you your whole life. You didn't get the good things in your life on your own; rather, the Creator of the universe is looking after you and opening doors. Scripture says that *"Whatever is good and perfect is a gift coming down to us from God our Father..."* (James 1:17). You are surrounded and pursued by God's goodness, and any good thing in your life is a gift straight from Him. Don't lose your amazement and awe at what God has done, and don't be fearful for the future. Look back over the good, perfect, precious, and wonderful things in your life and give thanks for God's goodness now and forever.

61

You are
a mighty hero.

Look to His Word:

The angel of the LORD appeared to him and said, "Mighty hero, the LORD is with you!"

JUDGES 6:12

See it for yourself:

You may feel weak, insecure, or unqualified, but don't let your feelings determine your identity. Look instead at what God says. He calls you a mighty hero. He calls you a giant-killer. He calls you a history-maker. It doesn't matter where you come from or what you've done. When we first meet Gideon in the Bible, he is hiding in a winepress! But God called him out just like God is calling you out — you too have greatness in you. You are a leader. You have so much potential in you. Don't disregard yourself. Don't become stuck in an old version of yourself. God has destined you to step up and leave your mark. You are not a side character or a background extra. You are a mighty hero.

02

You are *a light of the world.*

Look to His Word:

"You are the light of the world. A town built on a hill cannot be hidden."

MATTHEW 5:14 (NIV)

See it for yourself:

There are people who may never listen to a sermon or visit your church, but they're watching how you live, how you react to difficulties, and how you love others. When you live a life of excellence and integrity, day in and day out, when you're friendly and joyful and encouraging and wise, you are a bright light in a dark world. When you bring peace and a smile into every room, you are a city on a hill. People should want what you have. Don't add to the darkness. Don't hide your light. Do the right thing even when the wrong thing is happening. Be respectful even when they're disrespectful. God sees your light. Let it shine brightly in your workplace, your home, and your neighborhood.

You are sustained by God.

Look to His Word:

"So do not fear, for I am with you; do not be dismayed, for I am your God. I will strengthen you and help you; I will uphold you with my righteous right hand."

ISAIAH 41:10 (NIV)

See it for yourself:

When you feel completely overrun or like you can't go any further, remember this promise: You are sustained by the living God. One day you'll look back and say, "How did I survive that time?" And you'll know that God gave you the grace to get through it. He gave you the strength to outlast. He pushed back the forces of darkness and kept you from getting discouraged or giving up. He sustained you. Instead of complaining that your miracle is taking longer than you thought or that God hasn't come through yet, have a new perspective — God is sustaining you and giving you everything you need to keep moving forward. Sometimes God will rescue you from the fire, and other times God will stand with you through it. In either instance, do not be afraid. He will uphold you.

You are
promised rest.

64

Look to His Word:

Then Jesus said, "Come to me, all of you who are weary and carry heavy burdens, and I will give you rest."

MATTHEW 11:28

See it for yourself:

Life is full of things that steal our peace and rest, but Jesus promises to give you that which the world wants to take away. Rest isn't just about going on vacation once a year. God knows your body, mind, and spirit need consistent time to refresh and refocus. He knows you need good sleep and nourishing food. He knows you need uplifting community. He knows you need peace of mind and purpose. Remember, Jesus was human too. The Lord sees your hard work and downtrodden days and says, "Come to Me, and I will give you what you need to rest." Taking hold of this promise of rest is a two-way street though — you need to go to Him. He may ask you to spend extra time in His Word or draw boundaries with others, but take a deep breath; His promises are true. He will do what He says He will.

You are
free from condemnation.

Look to His Word:

So now there is no condemnation for those who belong to Christ Jesus.

ROMANS 8:1

See it for yourself:

The enemy works tirelessly to try to make you feel guilty and condemned by your mistakes. He wants to keep you emotionally drained, worn out, focused on your failures, and delayed from pursuing your destiny. But Scripture says there is no condemnation for those in Christ Jesus! Be bold and declare in faith that while you may not be perfect and while you may not feel worthy, you are saved by grace. When you gave your life to Christ, you became a new person. Through Christ, you can exchange guilt for grace and condemnation for peace. The Creator of the universe has made you blameless in His sight. This is a new day, and God wants you to live it free and without fear.

You are God's treasured possession.

Look to His Word:

For you are a people holy to the LORD your God. Out of all the peoples on the face of the earth, the LORD has chosen you to be his treasured possession.

DEUTERONOMY 14:2 (NIV)

See it for yourself:

Think about the earth and all the magnificent sights in it — sunsets and sunrises, swaying palm trees and glistening water, clouds over snow-capped mountain ranges. Think of the solar system — galaxies and stars and supernovas. God created it all and said it was good, but His most valuable and prized creation is you. You are the one He is the most proud and fiercely protective of. His only Son paid for your life with His own, and through Christ, you are now part of His chosen people. He says, *"You will be my people, and I will be your God"* (Jeremiah 30:22). You belong to Him, and He loves every little thing about you. You are a treasure to Him, more cherished and dear than all the gold in the world.

You are *not alone in your struggles.*

Look to His Word:

This High Priest of ours understands our weaknesses, for he faced all of the same testings we do, yet he did not sin.

HEBREWS 4:15

See it for yourself:

The enemy wants you to feel like you alone are struggling with a certain sin or problem or temptation, but that is a lie. *"The temptations in your life are no different from what others experience . . ."* (1 Corinthians 10:13). Difficulties come to every man and woman alive. No one is exempt. No one has a "get out of trouble free" card. And although He did not sin, even Jesus experienced temptation and trouble. You are not alone. Ask God how to defeat the temptation or struggles that come your way. The problem or temptation itself may not go away, but God will not allow it to be more than you can stand (1 Corinthians 10:13). He will show you a way out and help you overcome. With every struggle, difficulty, or temptation, you can boldly approach the throne of God and receive mercy, strength, and victory.

68

You are *being transformed.*

Look to His Word:

. . . Let God transform you into a new person by changing the way you think.

ROMANS 12:2

See it for yourself:

You can be a victorious and free person — confident and secure, brave and creative, disciplined and focused. But this doesn't just happen automatically. You have to be transformed, like a caterpillar changes its form and is released from its cocoon as a butterfly. How does this happen for you? Scripture says God transforms you through the renewing of your mind. Changing your thoughts is what changes you into who God created you to be. When your thoughts are condemning and saying, "I can't change. This will never get better," remind yourself of God's Word and what He says about you. Reprogram your thinking by agreeing with Him. And every day that you think the right thoughts, you're breaking out of that cocoon a little bit more. Before long, you'll be soaring like a butterfly to places you've never dreamed of.

You are
blessed when you persevere.

Look to His Word:

Blessed is the one who perseveres under trial because, having stood the test, that person will receive the crown of life that the Lord has promised to those who love him.

JAMES 1:12 (NIV)

See it for yourself:

Sometimes you have to endure through tears to get to the joy . . . or through pain to get to the blessing. Life isn't always fair, but seasons of trial and testing have purpose, and if you keep being faithful, even through difficult times, you're going to see what God's been working on. Scripture even says to *"consider it pure joy . . . whenever you face trials of many kinds"* (James 1:2, NIV). This is because you are blessed when you persevere through trouble. Perseverance produces character and hope (Romans 5:3–5), and it prepares you for the future God has planned for you. You are able to endure. And as you persevere, you will become who God created you to be. Trials are the proving ground for great blessings in your life.

70

You are welcomed into His presence.

Look to His Word:

Now we can come fearlessly right into God's presence, assured of his glad welcome when we come with Christ and trust in him.

EPHESIANS 3:12 (TLB)

See it for yourself:

When you approach God, He is thrilled. He is a good Father who loves to be with His children. Every time you open your Bible or sit down to pray or worship Him in church, He smiles. He loves when you take time in His presence, sharing your concerns and dreams. Many people have an inaccurate view of God — that He's harsh or mad or vindictive. But God always has the "Welcome" mat out. And because of your faith in Christ and His sacrifice, you can approach God with boldness and confidence (Hebrews 4:16). Not because of your good works but because you're His child. Don't let a wrong image of God or guilt or shame keep you from Him. God has already forgiven you. He doesn't expect you to have your life together. You can come just as you are *". . . fearlessly right into God's presence, assured of his glad welcome . . ."* (Ephesians 3:12, TLB).

You are a co-worker with God.

Look to His Word:

For we are co-workers in God's service; you are God's field, God's building.

1 CORINTHIANS 3:9 (NIV)

See it for yourself:

You are invited to participate in something so much bigger than yourself. It doesn't matter what your past looks like or how many mistakes you've made; Scripture calls us all co-workers or co-laborers in God's service. You have a divine job. Jesus said that the harvest is plentiful, but the workers are few (Matthew 9:37). Will you answer the call to work alongside Christ? With every act of kindness or word of encouragement or step of faith, no matter how small, you are working with God to bring the Good News of salvation to everyone and positively impact those around you. You are a vital part of God's Kingdom, and He has equipped you with gifts and talents to share the love, hope, and Good News of Jesus to the world. Lift up your head to the fields — the harvest is plenty.

72

You are *held in God's hands.*

Look to His Word:

"See, I have engraved you on the palms of my hands; your walls are ever before me."

ISAIAH 49:16 (NIV)

See it for yourself:

You are a big deal to God. Your name is tattooed on the palm of His hand. He knows everything about you. He even knows what you'll do before you do it. You are held safely and securely. You belong to Him, and He is committed to supporting you, sustaining you, guiding you, and protecting you from harm. You can navigate this life with confidence because you are never out of God's sight. Your face is always before Him. In times of uncertainty or difficulty, you can be at peace because you are cradled by God's steady and mighty hands. There, He nurtures you with care and compassion, giving you everything you need to face this world and accomplish the assignment He has purposed for you.

You are
a beacon of hope to others.

Look to His Word:

May the God of hope fill you with all joy and peace as you trust in him, so that you may overflow with hope by the power of the Holy Spirit.

ROMANS 15:13 (NIV)

See it for yourself:

Weeping may endure for a night, but joy is coming. You may be overflowing with doubt, with discouragement, with worry, but God wants you to overflow with hope. The odds may be against you, but don't stop believing. You may not see a way, but keep thanking God that He has one. Keep believing, despite what your circumstances look like, and hope will spring up within you. Keep thanking God rather than whining, and keep expecting things to change in your favor. Then you'll see God create a miracle in your life. And others will notice it as well. Your hope will be contagious. It will be a beacon for others around you. As you overflow with hope, declaring God's faithfulness in the past, present, and future, you will bring hope to everyone around you.

You are
a valuable part of your community.

Look to His Word:

Carry each other's burdens, and in this way you will fulfill the law of Christ.

GALATIANS 6:2 (NIV)

See it for yourself:

You were brought into your family, your circle of friends, your work environment, your church, and your neighborhood for a purpose. Nothing is an accident. God has placed you there to serve and be a light. And He sees every act of kindness. He sees you volunteering at the hospital or at church. He sees how you encourage and care for your co-workers. People may not notice all you do, but God does. Having a great life doesn't just come from success, from a nicer car, or material things. It comes from people — investing in and caring about those around you, even when they don't acknowledge or appreciate you. It comes from being a great friend, family member, employee, and neighbor. You are a valuable and vital part of your community, and as you carry others' burdens and serve them, you fulfill God's call.

You are
part of God's divine plan.

Look to His Word:

In him we were also chosen, having been predestined according to the plan of him who works out everything in conformity with the purpose of his will.

EPHESIANS 1:11 (NIV)

See it for yourself:

You are part of something bigger. God has a divine purpose for your life, and He is in control. He is lining up everything, to the smallest detail, to accomplish His plan. You may have made big mistakes in the past — and perhaps you continue to make them — but that's not a surprise to God. He has already calculated all your flaws and failures into your destiny. Nothing can stop what He has ordained. An accident cannot stop God's plan. Nor can someone else's attacks against you. You don't have to live worried or stressed. You don't have to force things to happen. All you have to do is keep God in first place. Honor Him with your life, and His divine plan will come to pass.

76

You are *creative.*

Look to His Word:

And he has filled him with the Spirit of God, with wisdom, with understanding, with knowledge and with all kinds of skills— to make artistic designs for work in gold, silver and bronze.

EXODUS 35:31-32 (NIV)

See it for yourself:

You were made in God's image, and God is creative! Therefore, He has placed in you the ability to create new, resourceful, imaginative, artistic, and purposeful things. He has given you the ability to creatively solve problems and develop programs and invent products that will positively impact your world. Whatever field you are in — medicine, sales, construction, accounting, teaching, raising children, ministry — ask God to help you open your mind to God-sized possibilities and ideas. He will give you ideas, designs, inventions, algorithms, songs, books, and ways to solve problems that are unique and will stand out. There's no limit to what God can do in you and through you to help others. In Him, you are endlessly creative because there's no limit to His ingenuity, imagination, and knowledge.

77

You are
a warrior.

Look to His Word:

Therefore, put on every piece of God's armor so you will be able to resist the enemy in the time of evil. Then after the battle you will still be standing firm.

EPHESIANS 6:13

See it for yourself:

Scripture says we are in a battle, not against flesh and blood, but against evil. Thankfully, we are not left defenseless. God has given you armor to wear — the belt of truth, the breastplate of God's righteousness, the shoes of peace that bring the Good News, the shield of faith, the helmet of salvation, and the sword of the Spirit, which is God's Word (Ephesians 6:14–17). You can approach any battlefield as a soldier of Christ (2 Timothy 2:3), knowing that while you are in God's armor, He is by your side, allowing you to resist the enemy. You can fight against evil with ferocity and strength. When you have this warrior mentality, an attitude of faith, and the knowledge that you are fully equipped through Christ, then all the forces of darkness cannot stop you. No weapon formed against you can prosper. No battle is too tough for you and God together. You will be found standing firm.

78

You are *chosen to bear fruit and be fruitful.*

Look to His Word:

"You did not choose me, but I chose you and appointed you so that you might go and bear fruit . . ."

JOHN 15:16 (NIV)

See it for yourself:

We all go through seasons where nothing is improving or growing, where we feel limited or tested, and it's easy to become discouraged. In those times, keep obeying God. Keep doing what He says. You are called, chosen, to bear fruit, and as you stay rooted in your faith and refrain from become weary in doing good, you will bear the fruit of the Spirit and show God's character to a lost world. You may not see growth, or you may feel limited for a season, but your time is coming. You are fruitful, you are prosperous, and you are growing. God will cause you to flourish in His perfect timing, and the fruit of your season will honor Him, testify to His love and provision, and fulfill His purposes for your life.

79

You are
a joy to God.

Look to His Word:

"For the LORD your God is living among you. He is a mighty savior. He will take delight in you with gladness. With his love, he will calm all your fears. He will rejoice over you with joyful songs."

ZEPHANIAH 3:17

See it for yourself:

Every day when you get up, God is happy to see you. He loves to hear your voice and see your heart focused on Him. Like a proud Father, you give Him so much joy! Each step you take in your faith brings a smile to His face. He sings joyful songs over you and celebrates your very existence. He's in the front row cheering for all your victories, and when you turn to Him in tough times, He's at your side fighting your battles, comforting you, and bringing you peace. You never bother or annoy Him with your prayers — He never rolls His eyes at you. You are His beloved child, and all He wants is to spend time with you.

You are guided by the Lord.

Look to His Word:

I will instruct you and teach you in the way you should go . . .

PSALM 32:8 (NIV)

See it for yourself:

God wants to guide you in every area of your life — not only the big things. He wants you to share the details of your everyday world with Him, and He wants to guide you through it all. You may feel like your life is uncertain or the path ahead is dark, but God's Word is a lamp for your feet and a light for your path (Psalm 119:105). As you acknowledge Him and seek His will in all you do, He will show you what path to take and what moves to make (Proverbs 3:6). Establish Him as part of your everyday life, and He will connect all the dots. You may not understand everything along the way, but you can be sure that God knows what He's doing. As you listen to Him, He will guide you.

You are meant to thrive and not just survive.

Look to His Word:

"... I have come that they may have life, and have it to the full."

JOHN 10:10 (NIV)

See it for yourself:

God doesn't just give you what you need to survive; He always provides more than you need. He is a God of overflowing abundance and blessing. When Jesus fed the five thousand, there wasn't an exact amount of bread and fish — but there were twelve baskets left over. And there were leftovers on purpose. He is a more-than-enough God. He wants you to thrive so everyone knows how good He is. Quit having a survival or scarcity mindset. Don't just pray to get by or endure. Dare to pray big prayers. Ask Him for your dreams, for success, and for overabundant increase. He can do exceedingly, abundantly more than we can even ask (Ephesians 3:20). Jesus came that you may have life to the fullest. You are meant to truly thrive.

You are *destined for greatness.*

Look to His Word:

And we know that in all things God works for the good of those who love him, who have been called according to his purpose.

ROMANS 8:28 (NIV)

See it for yourself.

You may feel insignificant, like you could never make much out of your life, but you were destined for greatness. It doesn't matter where you went to school or what your family is like or what giants are ahead. People may look down on you, but don't let that hinder you from your destiny. God approves of you, and He has planted the seeds of greatness within you. The struggles or setbacks you have been through haven't disqualified you. They have prepared you for what's next. God is working for your good. Don't shrink back or talk yourself out of the dreams He has placed inside you. You have an important assignment in His Kingdom. He will open doors no person can shut and give you success in seemingly impossible things. Follow God, and He will help you into your great purpose.

83

You are *strengthened in weakness.*

Look to His Word:

"... My grace is sufficient for you, for my power is made perfect in weakness."

2 CORINTHIANS 12:9 (NIV)

See it for yourself:

God knows what you're up against. He knows when you feel exhausted and weak and ready to give up. He sees what's not fair. He sees the disappointments, the lonely nights, and the struggles you try to hide. And when you invite Him into these tough moments, He will provide supernatural strength and power to do what you could not do on your own. Scripture says that *". . . those who trust in the LORD will find new strength. They will soar high on wings like eagles. They will run and not grow weary. They will walk and not faint"* (Isaiah 40:31). So trust in the Lord and get ready; special strength is coming your way. In your weakness, you are strong.

You are
given wisdom.

Look to His Word:

If you need wisdom, ask our generous God, and he will give it to you. He will not rebuke you for asking.

JAMES 1:5

See it for yourself:

Every day, you have choices to make about your life, your family, your job, your finances, your friends, and your home. And sometimes it's just difficult to know which way to go. Perhaps you are overwhelmed or confused. The good news is that you are not left alone in these decisions. The enemy operates in confusion, but God wants to provide wisdom and guidance. All you need to do is ask Him, and He is faithful to generously pour out wisdom upon you. He will give you clear direction and revelation to apply to your life. Read God's Word and trust in Him as your wonderful counselor (Isaiah 9:6). He is the greatest therapist and guidance counselor of all time. Invite the Holy Spirit into your decisions, acknowledge Him in all your ways (Proverbs 3:6), and He will teach you and lead you to make wise and successful choices.

You are
not defined by your past.

Look to His Word:

. . . Forgetting what is behind and straining toward what is ahead.

PHILIPPIANS 3:13 (NIV)

See it for yourself:

Your past may be filled with very real pain and sin, but that does not cancel out the destiny God has planned for you. He knows every thing you've ever done and every hurtful thing that's happened to you, and He has still called you and set you apart for His purposes. It's time to forget the guilt, shame, and pain of the past. It's time to move forward. You are not defined by the things you've done or by the things that have been done to you. Say no to the negative labels the enemy wants to place on you — he does not get to name you. God has forgiven you, healed you, and redeemed you. Your identity and your past, present, and future belong to Him. You are wiser and stronger because of what's behind, and God is preparing you for great things ahead.

86

You are *righteous.*

Look to His Word:

For if, by the trespass of the one man, death reigned through that one man, how much more will those who receive God's abundant provision of grace and of the gift of righteousness reign in life through the one man, Jesus Christ!

ROMANS 5:17 (NIV)

See it for yourself:

"Righteous" means holy, honorable, blameless, or in right standing with God. Righteousness is a gift through Jesus Christ for all who will receive it, and God sees you as being righteous before Him right now. This is not as a result of anything you could have done or because you have your act together but because of Christ's sacrifice on the cross. In fact, Scripture says all of our righteousness is like filthy rags (Isaiah 64:6) — meaning you can't do anything to earn it or deserve it. But God made Christ, who had no sin, bear sin for us, so that in Him we might become righteous (2 Corinthians 5:21). Through Christ, you are a holy, righteous, blameless, honorable, anointed, amazing child. Start receiving the gift.

You are given the mind of Christ.

Look to His Word:

"... Who can know the LORD's thoughts? Who knows enough to teach him?" But we understand these things, for we have the mind of Christ.

1 CORINTHIANS 2:16

See it for yourself:

You can have the same mind and the same attitude as Jesus Christ. He had many difficulties while He was on the earth, but He wasn't filled with anxiety. He had people betray Him, but He wasn't bitter. He was mocked, but He wasn't offended. He was tempted, but He didn't sin. His faith and theology were tested, but He didn't doubt. He trusted completely, loved completely, and followed through on His calling completely. As a follower of Christ and through the Holy Spirit, you are divinely empowered to think and act like Him. Through Him, you can understand Scripture, you can hear God's voice, and you can have the same thoughts as Jesus in any circumstance, for you have the mind of Christ.

You are surrounded by God's presence.

Look to His Word:

Where can I go from your Spirit?
Where can I flee from your presence?

PSALM 139:7 (NIV)

See it for yourself:

It's easy to be discouraged or afraid of trouble, sickness, debt, and the unknown, but the truth is, you are not surrounded by difficulty or evil; you are surrounded by the Most High God. You cannot escape His presence — Psalm 139 goes on to say that if you go up to Heaven, He is there, and if you go down to the grave, He is there. Even in the farthest oceans, God is there. Darkness itself cannot hide you from God. Your circumstances may look big, but you're surrounded by someone bigger. You have a hedge of protection around you, and God's presence is right by your side. The Holy Spirit is with you always — wherever you go, whatever you do — and He will protect you, guide you, deliver you, promote you, and empower you.

You are *storing up treasures in Heaven.*

Look to His Word:

"Do not store up for yourselves treasures on earth, where moths and vermin destroy, and where thieves break in and steal. But store up for yourselves treasures in heaven, where moths and vermin do not destroy, and where thieves do not break in and steal. For where your treasure is, there your heart will be also."

MATTHEW 6:19–21 (NIV)

See it for yourself:

With every good work — every generous gift, every kind word spoken, every person you've prayed for or helped — you are storing up for yourself treasures in Heaven. You may not see those treasures or be appreciated or thanked for them while here on the earth, but be assured that God sees every good deed, and He is counting them up. He sees how you love and care for people, and He is so proud of you. He sees when you give, even if it's in secret, and He will reward you (Matthew 6:4). You are known in Heaven, and you will be rewarded for your great faith and good deeds. So do not grow weary in doing good; in time you will reap a harvest (Galatians 6:9). When you are tired, keep this in mind: You are storing up great treasure.

90

You are *a source of encouragement to others.*

Look to His Word:

Therefore encourage one another
and build each other up . . .

1 THESSALONIANS 5:11 (NIV)

See it for yourself:

You are meant to encourage and comfort others, and you have exactly what someone else needs to make their life better. Someone out there needs your smile, your words of wisdom, your hugs, your talents. And as you encourage and lift up others, you are fulfilling part of your calling. Scripture says that God comforts us so we can turn around and comfort others in the same way (2 Corinthians 1:4). So be on the lookout for opportunities to be a blessing to someone else today. Perhaps it's someone in your family or at the grocery store. Maybe God will put a certain friend on your heart to text an encouraging note. You are purposed to brighten someone else's day.

You are *given new mercies every day.*

Look to His Word:

The steadfast love of the LORD never ceases;
his mercies never come to an end.

LAMENTATIONS 3:22 (ESV)

See it for yourself:

Every day when you wake up, God's mercy is there to greet you. It didn't run out the day before. You don't have to build up a stockpile before you can draw from it. His goodness, love, grace, and mercy are unlimited. The enemy will accuse you and tell you that you can't ask God for help because you're at fault for the mess you made or that God won't listen to you. But the enemy is a liar — you are God's child, fully forgiven and covered by mercy. When you cry to the Lord in your trouble, He won't leave you hanging. He will give you another chance. He will work things together for your good. God doesn't give us what we deserve . . . because certainly we deserve far less. But God is forgiving, and He always offers us His mercy.

You are
being renewed day by day.

Look to His Word:

That is why we never give up. Though our bodies are dying, our spirits are being renewed every day.

2 CORINTHIANS 4:16

See it for yourself:

Life may be exhausting, disappointing, or just downright hard right now, but do not give up. Do not lose heart. Scripture never promised that you wouldn't experience suffering in this life, but you can still have hope. Through faith, you have access to eternal things. Quit focusing on your current burdens and problems. Embrace an eternal perspective, and your spirit will be renewed day by day. Begin to walk closer with God, and each day will become a new gift filled with grace, potential, and joy. No matter what is going on in your life, through Christ, you can face each day with peace and purpose. You can rejoice! He is living water — a fresh fountain that will restore and refresh even the most exhausted and downtrodden. He gives life to your bones and renews your soul every time you call on Him.

You are
both courageous and brave.

Look to His Word:

The wicked flee though no one pursues,
but the righteous are as bold as a lion.

PROVERBS 28:1 (NIV)

See it for yourself:

All courage comes from God. He has given you His Spirit and imparted within you supernatural strength, courage, and fortitude to go up against any obstacle or fear you may face in this life. Your difficulties may look scary, but you have God on your side! Scripture says, *". . . If God is for us, who can ever be against us?"* (Romans 8:31). You can be bold and brave in the face of any trial. Don't be frightened by how hopeless the situation looks or how dire your finances are or how bad the medical report is. Don't let fear win. You are bold as a lion. You are a man or woman of courage. Even if you are surrounded by trouble, you can be brave because the Lord is your light and your salvation; whom shall you fear? (Psalm 27:1).

You are
a recipient of God's promises.

94

Look to His Word:

And because of his glory and excellence, he has given us great and precious promises. These are the promises that enable you to share his divine nature and escape the world's corruption caused by human desires.

2 PETER 1:4

See it for yourself:

The Scripture says in Isaiah 55:11 that God's Word always produces fruit. It's always effective. Therefore, when you declare God's promises, straight from His Word, you can't be defeated. Through Christ, all of God's promises are fulfilled and guaranteed. They can't be refuted. You can have complete confidence in what He has promised you, regardless of your outward circumstances. He will not withhold good things from you (Psalm 84:11). When you face difficult times or you feel discouraged, declare what God says about yourself and your situation. Keep God's Word in your heart and on your tongue. The enemy loves to make loud threats and shout blatant lies, but you are a child of the Most High God and a full recipient of all the good promises in His Word.

You are
beautiful.

> ## Look to His Word:

Keep me as the apple of your eye;
hide me in the shadow of your wings.

PSALM 17:8 (NIV)

See it for yourself:

You are beautifully designed — your smile, your eyes, your laughter, your spirit. You are stunning. God created you with intention, and He said, "This is good." He fashioned you in His image, with intricate detail, and He loves to look upon you. God's creativity knows no bounds, and His standard of beauty goes beyond what people see and what the current culture says. It's not about the trendy clothes you wear or how you present yourself (although God wants you to take care of yourself with excellence); it's your inner self, who you are as a person, that is beautiful and of great worth in God's sight (1 Peter 3:3–4). Let God's truth transform how you view yourself and others. Walk with confidence, and your beauty will shine all the brighter.

You are *uniquely talented, gifted, and skilled.*

Look to His Word:

Each of you should use whatever gift you have received to serve others, as faithful stewards of God's grace in its various forms.

1 PETER 4:10 (NIV)

See it for yourself:

It's tempting to look at talented people and think, *I wish I had their talent! I wish I could do the things they do.* But here's the truth — what God has given other people would not work for you. You can try to be like someone else, but it won't go well because you were created to be you. God formed you with exactly the talents and gifts He wanted you to have, and He wants you to faithfully steward those gifts and use them to serve others. You are uniquely skilled to do something important in God's Kingdom and serve the people around you. So hone your skills, embrace your talents, and don't hide your gifts. Walk with confidence today that you have exactly what God created you to have.

You are
lacking nothing.

Look to His Word:

The LORD is my shepherd, I lack nothing.

PSALM 23:1 (NIV)

See it for yourself:

It can be easy to think that if you had more — more money, a bigger home, more talent, more friends — you would be happy or satisfied or able to pursue your dreams. But it's time to shift your outlook. As you honor God and seek Him, you will lack nothing. He will bring the talent, the connections, the resources, the energy, and the time you need to accomplish all He has for you. The Scripture says those who trust in the Lord will lack no good thing (Psalm 34:10). He will give you what you need when you need it. He will lead you beside still waters and green pastures; He will guide you, comfort you, and give you strength (Psalm 23). Don't waste energy worrying about the future. Quit making excuses and feeling intimidated. God will give you all that you need for this season.

You are *a work in progress.*

Look to His Word:

Being confident of this, that he who began a good work in you will carry it on to completion until the day of Christ Jesus.

PHILIPPIANS 1:6 (NIV)

See it for yourself:

Y̲ou do not need to be perfect. You do not need to have it all together. God does not require perfection; He desires dependence. And you can be confident that the work He began in your heart and life when you first believed in Him will be brought to completion. He will not leave you hanging. He will not leave you stuck. His power and grace are more than enough for every stage of your walk with Him. Do not let the enemy make you think you should be further along in your spiritual walk, health journey, relationships, job, or family. Do not let the enemy drag you down with shame or guilt. God delights in every bit of progress you make, and He is with you every step of the way.

You are *enough.*

> ### Look to His Word:

. . . So now I am glad to boast about my weaknesses, so that the power of Christ can work through me.

2 CORINTHIANS 12:9

See it for yourself:

When you look at what you have — your resources, your talent, your looks, your experience — it may not seem sufficient for the tasks ahead. Someone else always has more or better. But that's where God steps in. He can multiply what you have. He can take what looks insignificant and turn it into something extraordinary. With God by your side, everything you are becomes more than enough. So throw away your deficit mentality. You're not at a disadvantage. Quit being insecure. As you rely on God, He will fill in the spaces of your weaknesses and insufficiencies. In Christ, you are empowered to be more than strong enough, talented enough, and smart enough to do all He's called you to. In Christ alone, you become enough.

100

You are *accepted.*

Look to His Word:

Therefore, accept each other just as Christ has accepted you so that God will be given glory.

ROMANS 15:7

See it for yourself:

People may not accept you. They may demean you and treat you poorly. You may feel left out or forgotten or inferior. While that may hurt, you can rest in the truth that God accepts you. The Most High God, your Creator and defender, has accepted you. Did you know Jesus was rejected throughout His time on this earth? People spat on Him and turned away from Him and even nailed Him to a cross. He endured all that so you could be fully accepted by God. Your value and worth are not in anyone's hands but His. And as you walk in His acceptance, the Scripture says to accept others too. Your acceptance of others will be a witness of God's great love, and it will bring Him glory.

101 You are *growing every day.*

Look to His Word:

"Do not despise these small beginnings, for the LORD rejoices to see the work begin, to see the plumb line in Zerubbabel's hand. . . ."

ZECHARIAH 4:10

See it for yourself:

Your progress in life may seem slow or insignificant. You may feel like you're late or behind the curve. What God has given you right now may seem small, but with each move forward or baby step, you are growing and learning. Don't despise your small beginnings. Don't look to the left or to the right. Quit comparing your progress with others. You can't make yourself grow any faster than He has planned. You may not be where you want to be, but you can celebrate and enjoy the progress you have made. Be confident in what God has given you, and one day, He will take what looks like little and turn it into much. Keep pressing on. As you stay faithful and take steps to grow every day, you will see an overpouring of God's goodness, provision, and peace.

So we have come to know and to believe *the love that God has for us.* God is love, and whoever abides in love abides in God, and God abides in him.

1 JOHN 4:16 (ESV)

Closing Thought:

Believe it.
Speak it.
Repeat!